IN SUN, SNOW
TANKA FROM A WORLD OF SONG

A Tanka Anthology
in Memory of Linda Jeannette Ward

The British Haiku
Society

Founded 1990

Editor: A A Marcoff
Book layout and cover design: Iliyana Stoyanova
© **Cover artwork:** *a blue memory* – abstract
painting by Pamela A. Babusci

ISBN: 978-1-906333-19-5

Published by:
The British Haiku Society
16 Croft Gardens
Andover
Hampshire SP10 2RH
United Kingdom

Website: http://britishhaikusociety.org.uk/

Printed by:
Book Printing UK
Remus House
Coltsfoot Drive, Woodston
Peterborough PE2 9BF
United Kingdom

FOR LINDA: A TRIBUTE

In addition to being an award-winning poet, Linda Jeannette Ward was many things: by profession a psychologist working with judicial and educational institutions; by inclination a naturalist, an avid birder, an environmentalist, and an activist for the many causes in which she ardently believed.

Linda and her husband, jazz musician Skip Hancock, made their home in rural North Carolina not far from the Outer Banks. It was an environment where she could indulge her love of the natural world and find the raw material for expression in the beauty of her poetry.

Linda was my very dear friend, my sister-in-spirit. As I mourn her loss, I celebrate the joy and the wonder she brought to my life.

Jean Silverwood

INTRODUCTION

This anthology has been created as a tribute to the late tanka poet Linda Jeannette Ward. It showcases many fine contemporary tanka written by members of the British Haiku Society and poets from around the globe, and it has been made possible through the generosity of Linda's great friend, Jean Silverwood. On behalf of the BHS and all tanka poets, I should like to thank Jean very much indeed. Her personal statement about Linda appears in these pages.

As opposed to haiku, tanka express the world of the self: originally through aspects of being in love, like loss, hurt, longing and pain, but now more generally and broadly through many other aspects of being human: in relationships yes, but also in a whole range of experiences, in ways that cover the entire gamut of emotions and feelings. This means poems on any subject. Tanka often have a two-part structure – 'the poet sees', 'the poet reflects'. In the words of Joy McCall, tanka bring together inner and outer vision. James Kirkup once said, tanka are 'works of great beauty and exquisite sentiment', and wrote: 'Haiku strike a momentary chord. Tanka sing, and leave a lingering spell'.

In this modern world, people often seem more aware than ever of their emotions, and their relationships and feelings have become perhaps more complex and ambiguous and articulate. In such a milieu, tanka can sing to us from the depths of our being. They convey a whole lyrical universe – of emotion, thought, reflection.

Heidegger, who was passionately interested in poetry, wrote about 'Being-in-the-world', and this is what tanka focus on, and they can really move and thrill and connect. Linda Jeannette Ward was a tanka poet who truly showed her heart and soul, and she sings to us still across the years, across the oceans. Her poems strike me as miniature, yet infinite, gems:

> the comfort of tears
> mirrored in dragonfly eyes
> thousands of lives
> all at once in the sun
> pulling me into their dance

> sunlight trembles
> between the shadows
> of wind-capped waves...
> the way you caught my tears
> like stars between your fingers

Linda's tanka seem timeless, universal, and touch eternity. A few years ago, I had a brief correspondence with her and still possess her leaflet 'off center', signed to me 'in tanka friendship'. It contains this poem:

> for three dawns
> the faint call of tundra swans
> through a drifting mist –
> once more I replay your
> last message on my machine

So we now leave our poems, or messages, here on these pages in memory of a special, gifted soul, and may they sing and echo to us all, and leave 'a lingering spell'.

A A Marcoff

in the dark
a moon beam
catches a solitary figure
walking
in a crooked line

Addison Redley, UK

a prayer net
left behind
the echo
of sutras
in moonlight

ai li, UK

Amalia sings
from beyond the grave – unties
the knot in my heart,
then she sings one more fado
and ties it in knots again …

Alan Maley, UK

clouds above
a solar fountain
i wonder out loud
at your
on-off love

Alan Peat, UK

the mountain hare
changed its coat
to white
only this winter
the mountain didn't

Alasdair Paterson, UK

the wig
made out of her hair ...
her child
on a wheelchair
folds paper cranes

Alvin B Cruz, Philippines

music vibrates
from his Slovakian flute
the blue
of mountains far away
beyond my climbing

Amelia Fielden, Australia

your love
goes unseen
the snow
burying your letter
my only keepsake

Amoolya Kamalnath, India

each year
a little more of you
to love
a little more of me
to do the loving

Andrew Shimield, UK

in the middle
of the darkest
day
a glimpse
of goldfinch

Ann Rawson, UK

the first ferry boat
fading into
pink and purple clouds
my hands full of
last night's scent

Anna Yin, Canada

twilit take-off
its right then left leg
lifts the river
a great blue heron
is winging skyward

an'ya, USA

the promise
of spring rain
how I hope
something good comes
from all these tears

Bryan Rickert, USA

twilight
grains of sand
on the finger tips
the flight of a bird
leaves no trace

Carmela Marino, Italy

our
ever after
drifting
into song
into dawn

Caroline Skanne, UK

steam rising
from our coffee cups ...
silence
hangs in the air
of our hazy past

Chen-ou Liu, Canada

high summer
the roaring fall
a memory
old love
a trickle

Christa Pandey, USA

lifting slowly
behind white veil clouds
clear face of mount fuji
the sun awakens
the sleeping beauty

Christopher Calvin, Indonesia

her exquisite
tenderness of heart
in every touch
and word ...
gentle rain

Claire Vogel Camargo, USA

all day
at the shallow river
small sounds
go bending
over the stones

Colin Oliver, UK

in an old album
a young portrait of mother –
a whole different world
before my time, and
beyond my reach

Corine Timmer, Portugal

in the murmur
of a slow-moving river
a new dawn
she wipes tears
from her pillow again

C X Turner, UK

thinking of you
I wave my hands
over red salvias ...
moments later
a hummingbird arrives

Daipayan Nair, India

alone
on an uphill path
I breathe
the scented wind
of broom bushes

Daniela Misso, Italy

doors left
wide open revealing
an unlit space
nothing here to steal
but the darkness

David Bingham, UK

autumn colours
in the garden of remembrance
each tree bears a name
the dappled disappearance
of dusk

David J Kelly, Ireland

snowshoe tracks
enter a fury of white,
chain-linking
the past to present
to unknowable future

Debbie Strange, Canada

five magpies
stand in flowerpots
left barren by drought
rain splashes down
now six for gold

Derek Hughes, UK

a handful of petals
gathered by a little boy
now they're all that's left
of the golden rain tree
alchemy in a tin

Diana Webb, UK

hawk's shadow
pulls my eyes to the sky
a circle and turn
clouds and day moon
i too hunger for something

Eve Castle, UK

i don't know
what love is
only what life is like
without you
in it

Femi Akinyele, UK

like a grain
      of sand
that hurts
the heart of an oyster –
you became my pearl

Firdaus Parvez, India

voices in the night
depths of the universe
inside small skulls
her talk of us having met
in the Himalayas

Francis Attard, Malta

short walk –
at every step
your young face
and the splendour
of daffodils

Frank Williams, UK

inside me
a tsunami crashing
white rabbits
frolicking on the waves
nothing is solid

Genie Nakano, USA

in this hotel
sounds of the city
through my window
words I do not understand
stories I'll never know

Geoffrey Winch, UK

the tension
between us
a red kite's feather
illuminates
the hillside

Graham Duff, UK

pumpkin seeds ...
the small secrets shared
with a classmate
remembering his betrayal
my broken heart

Hassane Zemmouri, Algeria

the lotus flower
blooms in slush and mud
can I turn
this dank year of pain
into something good?

Hazel Hall, Australia

now's the time
to climb every mountain
find my inner Maria
sing farewell when the crows drop by
heads cocked to one side

Helen Buckingham, UK

potting mix
crumbling through
un-greened fingers
this summer of love
disentangling

Helen Gaen, UK

Tea again with mother
three years widowed now
each week I see
trees shed their leaves
show more of the hills beyond

Ian Storr, UK

late summer
sudden wind scatters
rose petals
I do miss your song,
little nightingale

Iliyana Stoyanova, UK

shedding a tear
under the pitch black sky
I remind myself
there's a fire in me
brighter than stars

Jackie Chou, USA

the first leaves
in equal measure
to dead wood ...
the warmth of your hands,
the sorrow in your eyes

Jim Chessing, USA

cardinal butterfly
trapped by the church
stained glass window
colours flowing
from wings to glass

Jim Curry, UK

Grant Park
a blanket of polyester
for her cardboard bed
I dream a song of crickets
serenading her

Jo Balistreri, USA

treacle brown water
rippling
over ancient stones
too soon
you fly away

Joan Gibson, UK

is this the answer
to a forgotten song
a woodland note
follows me deeper
into flight

Joanna Ashwell, UK

Buddha at peace
in snow, rain and heat –
tonight, the moon
has tears to shed ... the Buddha
too much at peace to ask why

John Gonzalez, UK

the sky is blue
the small clouds are white
the blackbird is singing
all the trees are green
... she has peace

Joy McCall, UK

new roles
grandma and grandad
one little boy
shines in our lives
like a supermoon

Julie Thorndyke, Australia

in the darkness
        a stirring
within lotus buds –
soon their secrets will open
to the rising sun

Kala Ramesh, India

does mother flutter
with you bluest of moons
out of her cocoon
the hourglass urn
is full of butterflies

Kath Abela Wilson, USA

the height of monsoon
forest mosquitoes swarm
breezy palm trees sway
as the warm rain soaks my skin
a slice of moon lights the sky

Katherine E Winnick, UK

old man stares
into memory –
    tugging web-threads,
the solitary moth
    flutters backward

Keith J Coleman, UK

autumn conference
a gift over dinner
postcard of Fujisan
another dharma brother
passed to the other shore

Kenneth Mullen, UK

crouching towards
the distant black buck ...
I turn my camera
to the rise
of a lapwing

K Ramesh, India

the pause
of the dragonfly
stops me midway ...
I think of the times
our silence stood between us

Lakshmi Iyer, India

news of her death
on the car radio ...
as tears trickle down
memories arise of the songs
she had sung

Madhuri Pillai, Australia

deep forest
wanders quietly
the silence
in his pace finds
a new path

Mallika Chari, India

I look for myself
under the moon shadow
I feel really lonely
will I find the sky of your eyes
at dawn again?

Maria Concetta Conti, Italy

breeze off the lake
I drift in and out
of love
I kiss the berry stains
on little fingers and toes

Marilyn Ashbaugh, USA

cathedral bells
toll midnight
haze
from a blues bar –
that stranger's kiss

Marilyn Fleming, USA

sun glints on silver
framing
a life distilled
to a photo
on my desk

Mark Boor, UK

the bullfinch
and his mate
never far away
they work as a team
a dream I once had

Mark Gilbert, UK

in a pile on the floor
sand, swimsuits, towels
and a single sea star ...
how did such beauty slip
unseen into my life

Mary Kendall, USA

only with you beside me
do I find peace
in the darkness
an ancient oak
cradles the moon

Maureen Edden, UK

over the estuary
the enormous gibbous moon
and wee gazing
in August drought
a white moth flutters

Maureen Weldon, UK

in the pages
of an old *National Geographic*
about australopithecus
from dad's collection
a cherry blossom

Michael Dylan Welch, USA

our first neighbor
shy in cape and fedora
passing with never a word
but we heard Bach deep in the night ...
the man I've become

Michael Flanagan, USA

this afternoon
a butterfly flutters
here and there ...
a few wildflowers bloom
in her unkempt garden

Milan Rajkumar, India

thoughts of you
when I was least expecting
winter rain
a peacock quickly jumps
onto the wall

Minal Sarosh, India

seaside walk
an ocean rages within me
around me ...
I long for the times
you held me close

Mona Bedi, India

I time travel –
Tamabe no Akahito*
and I watch
Fuji's jagged cone explode:
Heaven and Earth divided

Neal Whitman, USA

*Nara period poet of 8th century

my hands
caress the child's face ...
moonlight
on the flowing river
glows silvery blue

Neena Singh, India

billowing curtain
muffled car horn ...
grandma's lullabies
from childhood
louder than the rain

Neera Kashyap, India

news
of her death
i seem
to have lost my way
in this world

Pamela A Babusci, USA

the day we left
was made for surfers
sea rolling in
long, smooth combers
metal-grey to greenish-blue

Patricia Prime, New Zealand

meadow cranesbills ...
we tread forgotten paths
with our friend
pausing in awe
as we glimpse a rainbow

Paul Beech, UK

observing birds
how they move
through light and dark
bringing them closer
towards my soul

Paul Hickey, UK

all the hopes
and dreams
it awakens in me –
the almost not there
of a wren

Paul Smith, UK

gardening
in the flowered straw hat
she always wore
with every wild rose tamed
a better fit

Peggy Hale Bilbro, USA

in his shed
grandad relaxing
thoughts blossom
thinking chair
creaks

Peter Morriss, UK

her fate
lulls her to sleep
the stars
blanket her scars
the moon caresses her body

Pravat Kumar Padhy, India

barefoot on dewdrops
I gaze in the wet darkness
and wait for your sign –
from time to time a pale fruit
clings on a thin twig - the moon

Radu Şerban, Romania

looking long
at my wedding picture
i think how
i must have looked
that day in the mirror

Richa Sharma, India

a year older
again crossing
the shallow stream
long pauses
for mossy rocks

Richard L Matta, USA

awaiting the wave
that'll wash away empty hours
and endless longing
in this dead silence at sea
I'd like to tear down the sky

R K Singh, India

my frosted breath
says I'm alive
a smouldering fire
across the estuary
shimmerings from another world

Robert Smith, UK

the garden buddha
glistens in summer raindrops
and gladioli   still
my worn shoes follow
the goldfinch song

Roberta Beary, Ireland

I ask
shall we turn the holiday
into a honeymoon,
you frown then smile
say yes

Roger Noons, UK

ancient chants
lace the evening air
the faint tinkling
of cow bells ...
as they return home

Rupa Anand, India

over the graveyard
through this penetrating heat
a sudden cool breeze
    can my father hear it too
    the temple bell of Soja

Sean O'Connor, Ireland

turning wind ...
the desert sand
cannot reveal
how far we have travelled
though stars light our footprints

Shalini Pattabiraman, UK

what now
philosopher crow:
will you argue
with yourself
or the cerulean sky?

Sheila Windsor, UK

piano music
drifts from my neighbour
rising high
the flickering wings
of a late hunting swift

Simon Wilson, UK

episode
the man in the valley mist
i thought i knew
walking towards me
walking away

Steve Black, UK

flowers echo
children's laughter
in vibrant colours
small holi huts burn
under a crimson sky

Subir Ningthouja, India

we meet again
not knowing what to say
who will speak first?
a clash of waves
from different directions

Sue Richards, UK

a farmer
retilling his fields ...
if I had to
do it all again,
I'd still choose you

Susan Burch, USA

loosely arranged
in a glazed yellow vase
supermarket daffs
a homage
to Van Gogh

Susan King, UK

scream of vixen on a winter night
faint memory of something
I can't quite ...
perhaps one night
I'll remember

Sylvia Lees, UK

peak night
of the meteor shower
and clear skies ...
so pleasing another time
this full sturgeon moon

Taylor Jo Kelly, UK

mountain
cloud
memory will be
the orchid of my world
when it flowers like a dream

Tony Marcoff, UK

dawn
snow fall
a siren's wail
so deep
my prayer

Tony Nasuta, USA

rusty door handle
of the abandoned
parents' house
in the dollhouse
a stray puppy

Tsanka Shishkova, Bulgaria

a sliver
of day moon ...
saree slips
from the shoulder
of a nursing mom

Vandana Parashar, India

watching dozens
of blossoms settle in the urli*
I learn
the art of creating
    a space for myself

Vani Sathyanarayan, India

  *a decorative vessel used to float flowers

a single roe deer
in a forest clearing
stood there, staring over …
for a moment the world
is a less lonely place

Wendy Gent, UK

on the lip
of this homeless woman
a chapped flake of skin
begging to be freed
as last darkness closes in

Linda Jeannette Ward
(1947-2021)

Honourable mention in the 2020 BHS Awards

Index of Poets

• • •

• • •